D0688149

DIRT AND DESTRUCTION
SPORTS ZONE

DEMOLITION DERBY
TEARING IT UP

BRIAN HOWELL

Lerner Publications Company • Minneapolis

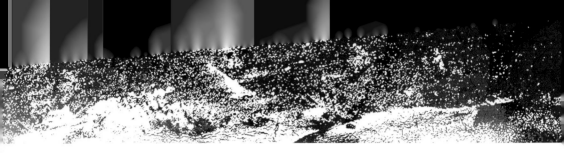

Lerner Publications Company
A division of Lerner Publishing Group, Inc.
241 First Avenue North
Minneapolis, MN 55401 U.S.A.

For reading levels and more information, look up this title at www.lernerbooks.com.

Content Consultant: Charlene Bower, Bower Motorsports Media

Main body text set in Folio Std Light 11/17.
Typeface provided by Adobe Systems.

The images in this book are used with the permission of: © Robert McGouey/Getty Images, p. 5; © Art Konovalov/Shutterstock Images, pp. 6, 10, 20, 22–23; © Action Sports Photography/ Shutterstock Images, p. 7; © ISC Archives/Getty Images, pp. 8-9; © Barbara J. Perenic/The Laramie Boomerang/AP Images, p. 11; © Lise Bennett/Shutterstock Images, pp. 12–13; © Jamie Roach/ Shutterstock Images, pp. 13, 18–19; © Tim Roberts Photography/Shutterstock Images, p. 14; © Daniel Horton/Havre Daily News/AP Images, pp. 16–17; © Kelly Humphrey/Brainerd Dispatch/AP Images, p. 17; © Shutterstock Images, p. 21; © Shawn Gust/Coeur d'Alene Press/AP Images, p. 24; © Danah Schremmer/iStockphoto, p. 25; © Jason Merideth/Shutterstock Images, p. 27; © The Washington Post/Getty Images, p. 28; © Vicki Smith/AP Images, p. 29.

Front cover: © Robert McGouey/All Canada Photos/Getty Images (main); © Janis Smits/ Shutterstock.com (background).

Library of Congress Cataloging-in-Publication Data
Howell, Brian, 1974–
    Demolition derby : tearing it up / by Brian Howell.
        pages   cm. — (Dirt and destruction sports zone)
    Includes index.
    ISBN 978–1–4677–2122–6 (lib. bdg. : alk. paper)
    ISBN 978–1–4677–2450–0 (e-Book)
    1. Demolition derbies—Juvenile literature. 2. Automobile racing—Juvenile literature. I. Title.
  GV1029.9.D45H68 2014
  796.7—dc23   2013018992

Manufactured in the United States of America
1 – VI – 12/31/13

TABLE OF CONTENTS

CHAPTER ONE

HISTORY OF DEMOLITION DERBY

Thirteen cars sat lined up around the wall of the arena. Their engines growled and roared as their drivers gripped the steering wheels. Suddenly green flags waved to signal the start of the derby. Drivers hit their gas pedals. The cars were off! Kicking up dirt with their tires, the cars took aim at one another.

A black car ran into the back of a blue car. *Smack!* The crash spun the blue car sideways. Seconds later, another car slammed into the side of the blue car.

For several minutes the old, beat-up cars took turns smashing into one another. The sounds of revving engines and crunching cars poured into the ears of the fans. They cheered loudly. Only one car was left running in the end. The rest of the cars were crushed and broken and unable to move.

The annual 2011 demolition derby at Greeley Stampede in Greeley, Colorado, was a hit with fans.

Demolition derby cars are built to crash and smash into other cars.

Greeley is not alone in its love of smashing cars. Hundreds of demolition derby events are held throughout North America, Europe, and Australia every year.

The idea of a demolition derby is simple. Drivers do all they can to smash the other cars and to be the driver who has the last car running.

BECOMING POPULAR

Demolition derbies began in the United States. But no one is sure exactly where or when the first one took place. Some say they were held at fairs as early as the 1930s.

Many people credit Don Basile for being the first to popularize the sport. In the 1940s, Basile bought four used cars and found four drivers. He set up an event at Carrell Speedway in Gardena, California. He wanted the cars to smash into one another.

РТЛАЙН
dasportline.ru

22

22

Певзнер А.

Demolition derby drivers do everything they can to protect their cars and to have the last car running.

Others believe it was Larry Mendelsohn who started the demolition derby trend. Mendelsohn was a stock car driver in Long Island, New York. Stock cars are cars that have been changed for racing. Mendelsohn crashed his car into a fence during a race that year. He quickly noticed fans were more interested in his crash than the race.

THE FIRST DEMO DERBY

We don't know where or when the first demolition derby was held. But we do know when the word was added to the English language. Merriam-Webster's Collegiate Dictionary lists circa 1953 as the first known use of the term demolition derby.

Mendelsohn helped popularize demolition derbies after seeing fans' reactions to stock car crashes.

"What this entire country is based on is the automobile," Mendelsohn said. "And people absolutely love to see them crash. Whenever there's an accident on a corner, you have a crowd gather around."

Mendelsohn bought a racetrack called Islip Speedway in Long Island, New York. He started holding demolition derbies there in 1958. Very few people had attended stock car races at Islip Speedway. But thousands of people showed up to watch demolition derbies.

Shortly after Mendelsohn brought the demolition derby to Islip Speedway, the sport gained national attention. Demolition derbies even spread around the world, with events in Europe and Australia.

Demolition derbies were a hit. The world had a new sport.

ISLIP SPEEDWAY

Islip Speedway is considered the birthplace of demolition derby. It is the most famous track in demolition derby history. During the 1960s, the track was featured many times on ABC. This allowed people around the United States to see the sport and become familiar with Islip Speedway. Islip Speedway was not just home to demolition derby events. Auto races of all kinds, including National Association for Stock Car Auto Racing (NASCAR) races, were held there. The track opened in 1947 and closed in 1984.

In addition to demolition derby races, Islip Speedway held many other auto races.

TELEVISED DERBIES

The ABC television network began airing demolition derbies on its popular *Wide World of Sports* show in the early 1960s. ABC paid approximately $2,000 for the rights to air the derby events at Islip. CBS bought the rights for $750,000 in 1975. Millions of people around the country tuned in to watch cars crunch into one another.

Demolition derby has lost much of its popularity on television in recent years. Since the 2000s, it is tough to find derby events on TV. But the sport has not died. All around the United States, derby events take place at county fairs and in towns such as Greeley.

SMASHING CARS FOR FANS

At the end of the 2011 Greeley Stampede derby, car parts sat in the dirt. Tires were ripped, and engines wouldn't run. The fans roared as the drivers got out of their cars and shook hands. The fans clapped even louder when the winner was named. Like so many derbies around the United States, this one gave fans all they wanted. And it proved that as long as there are old cars, people will want to smash them.

RULES AND STRATEGY

D emolition derby is a risky sport. Drivers wear protective gear during derbies to stay safe. They also make sure their cars are as safe as possible. And derby organizers set rules to help prevent drivers and fans from being injured. "The derby cars are built with the driver's safety in mind and the derby rules also focus on safe competition," said Ryan Sweat, who stars with his family in the TV show *Kings of Crash* on the Velocity channel.

Before getting into demolition derby cars, drivers dress properly. They wear long pants, long-sleeved shirts, helmets, and eye protection. Some drivers also wear fireproof suits.

Safety is also kept in mind when preparing cars for demolition derbies. Seat belts must be worn by derby drivers. All doors of a derby

car must be chained or welded shut. This means the doors won't open if the car is hit. The driver's door is also painted a different color or has a big white *X* on it. Derbies require windows to be removed so broken glass doesn't cut the drivers. Bars are often installed in place of the glass, which can stop any loose car parts from hitting the driver. Derby cars must also have at least one hole in the hood in case of an engine fire. The hole allows the fire to be put out faster.

The driver's door is painted differently so other drivers can easily see where they can't hit the car.

Track Rules

Different derbies have different rules. But there are a few basic rules followed in most derbies. Some rules state drivers must be at least 18 years old. Other derbies set the minimum driving age at 16 years old. Once the derby begins, drivers follow rules to stay safe and to ensure a lively competition. The first rule is cars must line up with their rear ends to

Most demolition derbies are held on an oval racetrack or in an oval arena.

the wall, facing one another before the start of the derby. This means all the cars start in a similar position. A second rule is drivers are not allowed to crash into another car's driver-side door. This rule helps prevent injuries to the drivers. The final rule is drivers are required to keep smashing into others as long as their cars can be driven. Some derbies require cars to make contact with another car every minute or two. This rule keeps the derby exciting and fast-paced.

A WINNING STRATEGY

It's important for drivers to know the rules of a derby. But it takes more than just knowing the rules to win a demolition derby.

"Everybody thinks it's pretty easy to just get in a derby car and go," said Robert Rice, who was a top derby driver in Southern California in the 1990s. "But there's skill involved. And luck. Definitely you have to be lucky."

FIGURE-EIGHT RACING

While most demolition derbies are held on an oval track, another popular form of derby racing is done on a figure-eight track. Sometimes two large truck tires are placed far apart on the track. Drivers then have to move around those tires in a figure-eight pattern. Other tracks have pavement in a figure-eight shape. The cars follow the figure-eight pattern and try to not crash. The car with the most laps completed wins.

Drivers must actively try to smash into other cars. Driver's don't want their engines to be damaged, so they try to avoid having the front of their cars hit. Some drivers use the back of their cars to smash into others. That way the trunk gets crunched and not the engine. But drivers can also avoid getting hit. One strategy is to keep themselves close to the wall with the driver's door facing the other cars. Because other racers are not allowed to hit the driver's door, this strategy helps drivers take fewer hits.

It is common to have a brightly painted wooden stick attached to a driver's door. When a driver's car is no longer running correctly, the driver breaks the wooden stick. This means the driver is out of the derby.

The winner of a demolition derby is determined by the last car running. A derby is made up of timed heats. A heat is one round of several in a competition. The heats lead up to the main event. The final demolition of the night is not timed. The derby ends when there is one car left running. Derbies can last up to 20 minutes depending on the number and quality of cars.

All three demolition derby drivers still have painted sticks attached to their doors. That means they are still participating in the event.

THE LARGEST DERBY

Most demolition derbies include about 12 to 20 cars. On March 16, 2002, a derby in New Zealand took derbies to another level. A total of 123 cars participated in a single race at Todd & Pollock Speedway in Mount Maunganui. One car finally emerged as the winner after 47 minutes of smashing and crashing.

Some demolition derby drivers use the rear of their cars to smash into other cars.

THE THRILL OF THE HIT

Demolition derbies are exciting events for drivers and fans in part because of the danger. But drivers can enjoy the thrill of a derby and stay safe at the same time. Robert Rice once broke his nose during a derby. But that is the only injury he suffered in more than 200 derbies.

"You think about [the danger]," Rice said. "But once you get in the car and you're seat-belted in, everything you're worried about totally goes away. . . .You might get butterflies before you go out. Some people do; some people don't. You know you're going to get hit."

That's one thing all drivers know going into a derby. They will get hit. They also hope to deliver a lot of hits. It's the thrill of those hits that keeps them coming back.

Accidents and injuries aren't very common at demolition derby events, but they can still happen.

CHAPTER THREE

DERBY CARS

Finding the right car is important for demolition derby drivers. Any old car can be driven into the arena to get smashed up. But it takes the right kind of car to win a derby.

Many drivers like to find cars made in the 1960s or the 1970s. Cars were made with heavy metals during those decades. These cars tend to survive crashes more easily. They can also deliver a lot of punishment.

Modern cars are made differently than cars from the 1960s or the 1970s.

Many demolition derby cars are found at junkyards.

JUNKYARD CARS

Demolition derby cars are from junkyards and don't cost much money. Drivers can find a great derby car such as a Chrysler Imperial from the 1960s or a Chevrolet from the 1970s. The goal is to find a vehicle that has a good structure and runs. The engine is the most expensive piece of the car.

There are different types of derbies. Some derbies use only trucks. Other derbies feature small cars. Some derbies even use old school buses.

SHORTAGE OF CARS

Thousands of demolition derbies have been held every year since the 1950s in the United States. At least 12 to 20 cars get battered at each derby. That's a lot of crunched vehicles! Some demolition derby drivers are finding it more difficult to find the types of cars they love to use. "We wrecked them all," said Sam Dargo, head of the International Demolition Derby Association.

BREAKDOWN OF A DEMOLITION DERBY CAR

PAINT JOB

Drivers paint their cars in many fun designs. If they are sponsored, the sponsor's logo is placed on the car. Some drivers also like to paint a number on their car. Most derbies require the driver's door to be painted a different color, too.

INTERIOR

The interior of the car is emptied of unnecessary parts. These parts include backseats, the carpet, wires, and even radio speakers. Taking parts of the car off makes the car lighter. Seat belts must stay in the car.

GAS TANK

Derbies require the stock gas tank to be removed. This is for fire safety reasons. Drivers typically put a plastic gas tank in the backseat for a derby.

OUTSIDE

Outside parts of the car are also taken off. This includes lights, chrome trim, and trailer hitches. Having fewer parts on the car makes it lighter, but also means less parts can be damaged. Drivers must fix or replace any parts that are damaged. Removing unnecessary parts means less work for the driver.

FIRE EXTINGUISHER

Drivers are required to have at least one fire extinguisher within reach. This is in case of a fire. A hole must also be cut in the hood of the car. This is in case of an engine fire.

DOORS AND WINDOWS

Doors are chained or welded shut. This prevents a door from opening when a car is hit. Windows are removed to prevent any broken glass. Some drivers use bars over the window space to prevent any loose car parts from coming in the car.

Demolition derby drivers decorate their cars with logos if they are sponsored by any businesses or organizations.

Robert Rice would spend as many as 70 hours getting a car ready for a demolition derby. All the work was done to make the car last as long as possible in the arena.

Drivers do one last thing to their cars before the vehicles are ready for demolition derbies. They paint them. Some drivers paint the car a single color. Others paint their cars in wild colors and fun designs. Some of the derby drivers have local sponsors. They paint the sponsor's logo onto the sides of their vehicles.

After a demolition derby is over, drivers have to spend time fixing their cars or decide to scrap them.

AFTER THE DERBY

At the end of a derby, the derby car goes home with the driver. The driver fixes the car to get ready for the next derby. Sometimes drivers have to scrap a car. This means the car can't compete anymore. Most drivers bring the car to a scrapyard. The scrapyard recycles the different car parts for money.

CHAPTER FOUR

DARING DRIVERS

A uto racing fans are very familiar with their favorite drivers. Jeff Gordon, Tony Stewart, Dale Earnhardt Jr., and many others are superstars in professional racing. Demolition derby drivers, on the other hand, aren't famous. Many of them are just average people looking for a thrill.

"Most of the people who have participated have always wanted to take an automobile and smack someone with it," said Frank Roberts, an organizer for Stoney Roberts Demolition Derby in the southern United States. "It's a controlled situation where you can do damage and destruction without hurting someone. It's adult bumper cars."

GREAT DEMOLITION DRIVERS

While demolition derby doesn't have famous drivers, it does have many great drivers. Ryan Songalewski won the USA Demolition Derby car championship for the third year in a row in 2012. It was his fifth championship in 11 years. In the 1990s, Robert Rice won most of the derbies he entered in Southern California.

SPEEDO

Ed "Speedo" Jager gained national attention in 2004 when PBS television filmed a documentary about him. Jager was featured in the film *Speedo: A Demolition Derby Love Story*. An auto mechanic, Jager is one of the nation's best derby drivers. He's also a husband and a father. In the film, Jager's son, Anthony, drives in his first derby.

Demolition derby drivers have the chance to crash their cars into other cars.

Demolition derby drivers aren't well known for the most part. They sign up for the simple joy of crashing a car. "You can smash your car without getting in trouble," said Eric Coss, who entered a demolition derby in New York's Delaware County when he was a teenager.

Some demolition derby drivers have been racing for years. Others, like Coss, are teenagers who recently learned how to drive a car.

The sport features mostly men, but several women drivers have participated and done well. Jen McMurphy made history at the 2012 Tillamook County Fair in Oregon. She became the first woman to win the demolition derby at the fair.

"I just love crashing into people," McMurphy said. "It's my first year, but ever since I grew up I loved coming to the demolition derby and watching the cars crash. I always wanted to do it, and it feels good winning."

Having fun crashing isn't the only quality of a good demolition derby driver. Drivers also have to love working on cars. Lynn Buchanan, from New York, spends many hours preparing his car for a demolition derby. He said it's a great way for him to relieve stress.

Demolition derby drivers spend a lot of time fixing up their cars.

An Expensive Hobby

Demolition derby drivers won't be bringing home a lot of money. Drivers usually spend more money on their cars than they could win in a derby.

Although drivers don't make much money at derbies, drivers provide fun moments for the fans and create priceless memories and stories that they love to share!

Fans enjoy the excitement and action that demolition derbies deliver.

29

GLOSSARY

FIREPROOF SUIT

a suit worn by demolition derby drivers to prevent them from being burned

FRAME

the main structure of a vehicle, also called a chassis

JUNKYARD

a location where old cars and car parts are stored

MECHANIC

a person who fixes cars

NASCAR

National Association for Stock Car Auto Racing; the organization that runs many professional races

SCRAPYARD

a place for receiving or handling scrap

STOCK

parts that come originally with a car

WELD

to put together metal by heating

FOR MORE INFORMATION

FURTHER READING

Howell, Brian. *Monster Trucks: Tearing It Up*. Minneapolis: Lerner Publications Company, 2014.

Lowenburg, Bill. *Crash Burn Love: Demolition Derby*. Stroudsburg, PA: Gazelle Distribution Trade, 2005.

WEBSITES

Demolition Derby
http://www.hartin.com

A veteran demolition derby driver provides tips and advice on how to succeed in the sport.

International Demolition Derby
http://www.internationaldemolitionderby.com

This site features photos and information on derbies held in the central part of the United States.

USA Demolition Derby Inc.
http://www.usademoderby.com

This is the official site for a demolition derby organization that has been around for nearly 40 years.

INDEX

ABOUT THE AUTHOR

Brian Howell is a freelance writer based in Denver, Colorado. He has been a sports journalist for nearly 20 years, writing about high school, college, and professional athletics. In addition, he has written books about sports and history. A native of Colorado, he lives with his wife and four children in his home state.